THE AMAZING WORLD OF SASSY MERMAIDS

An Adult Coloring Book

By

Karma Guru

THIS BOOK
BELONGS TO

_____

_____

_____

COLOR TEST PAGE

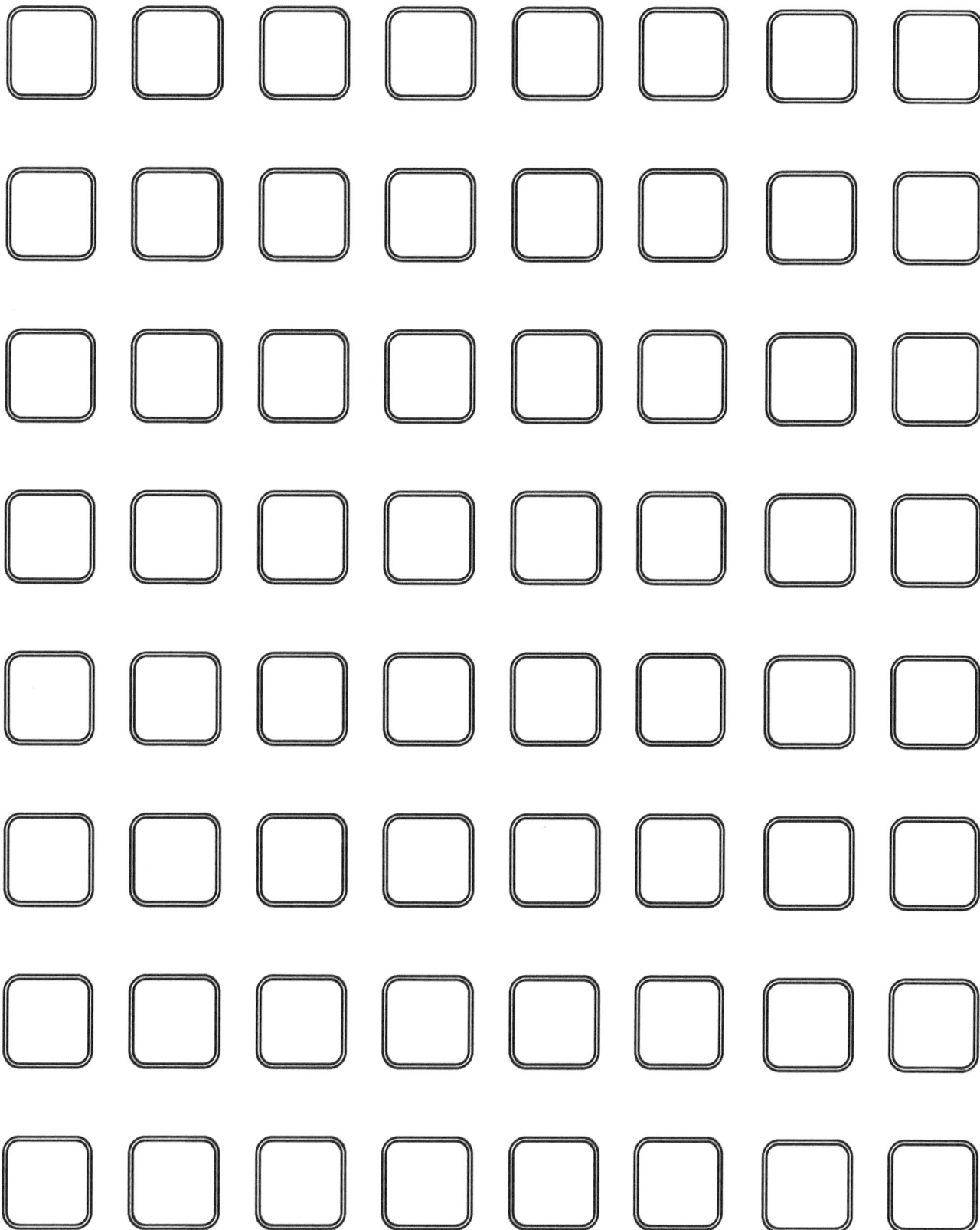

SUCK IT UP,
BUTTERCUP.

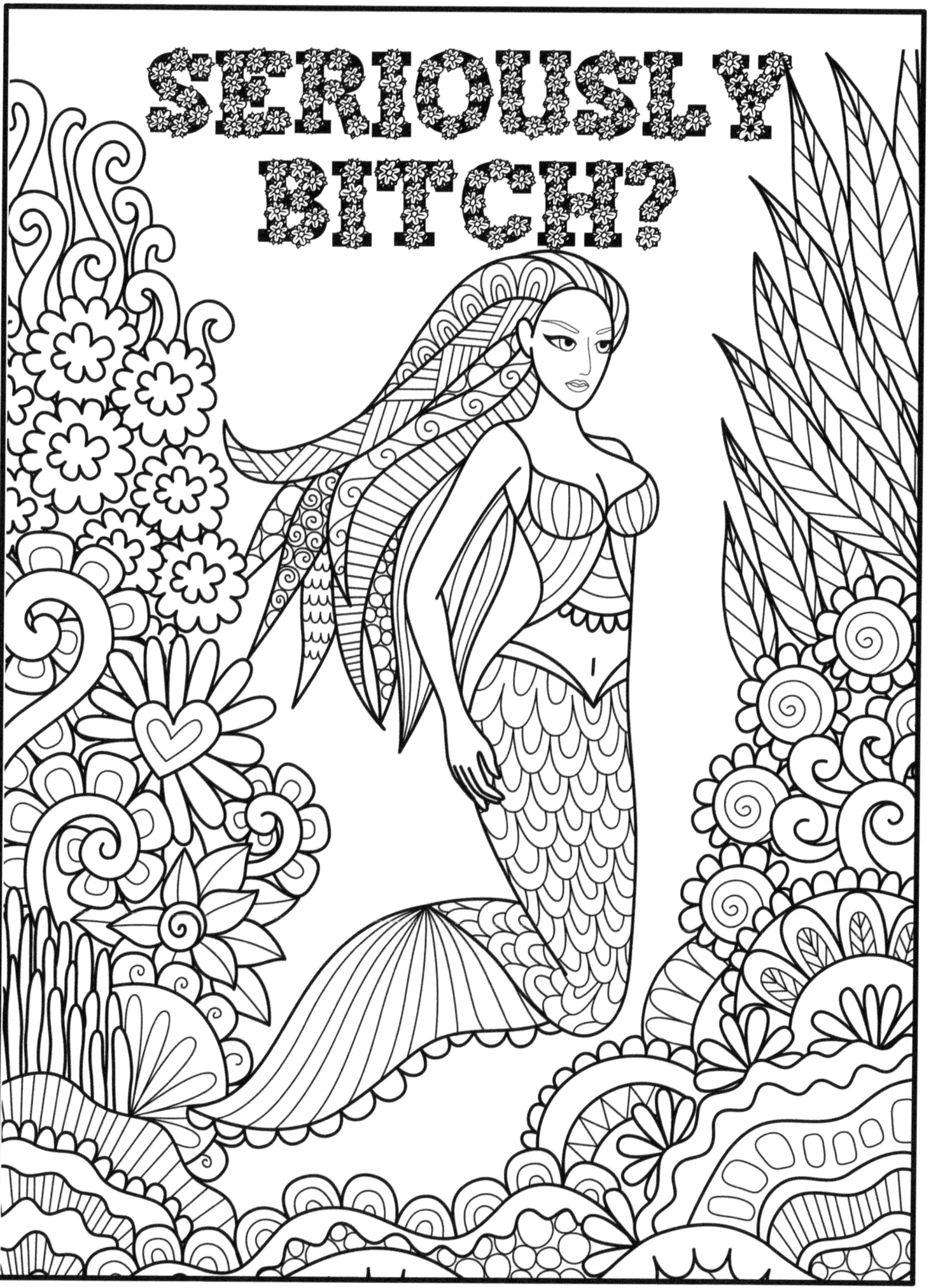

SERIOUSLY BITCH?

IF KARMA

DOESN'T HIT YOU, I GLADLY WILL.

Sunshine mixed with a little hurricane

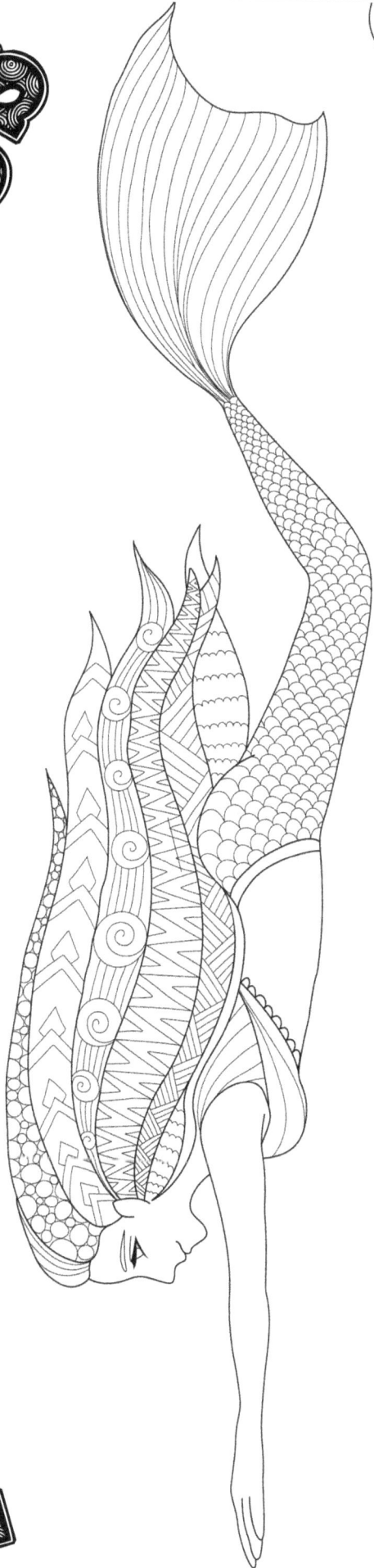

Be careful if you try to fill the world

OH DARLING, GO, BUY A GO, BUY A PERSONALITY

Your name is enough to piss me off

I'm just mean and people think I'm joking.

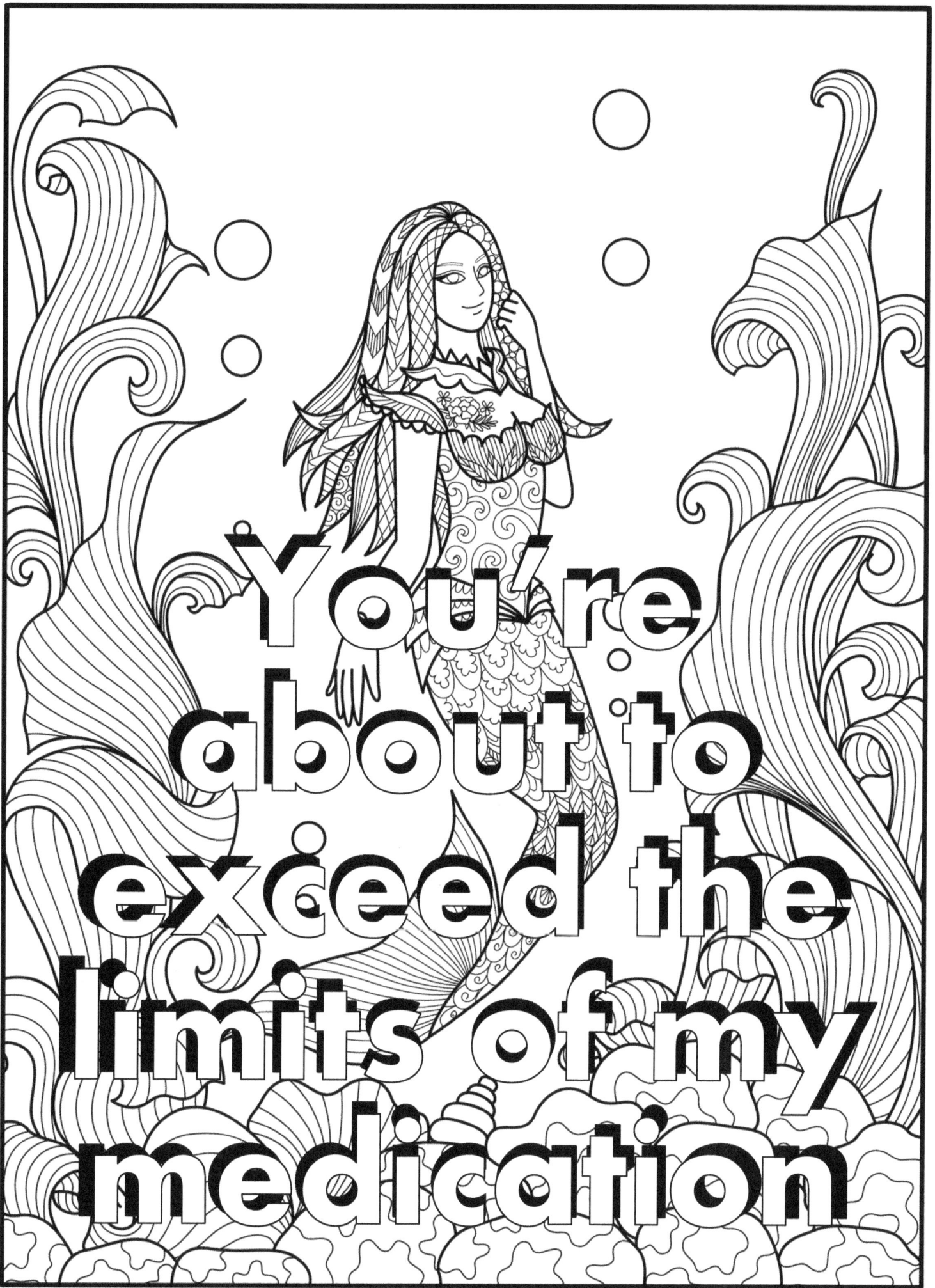

You're about to exceed the limits of my medication

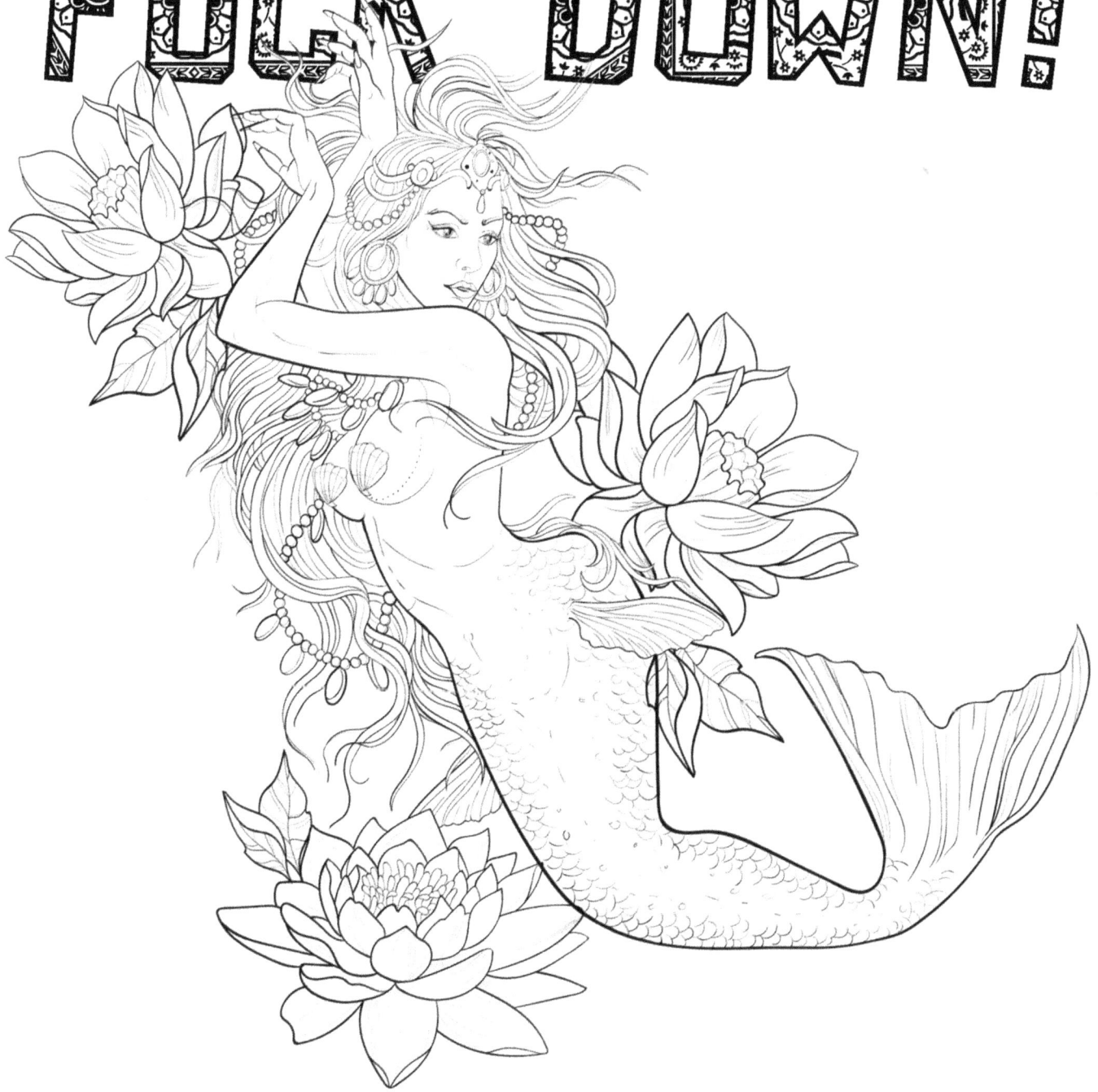

CALM THE FUCK DOWN!

SOME PEOPLE ARE SUCH TREASURES THAT YOU REALLY JUST WANNA BURY THEM.

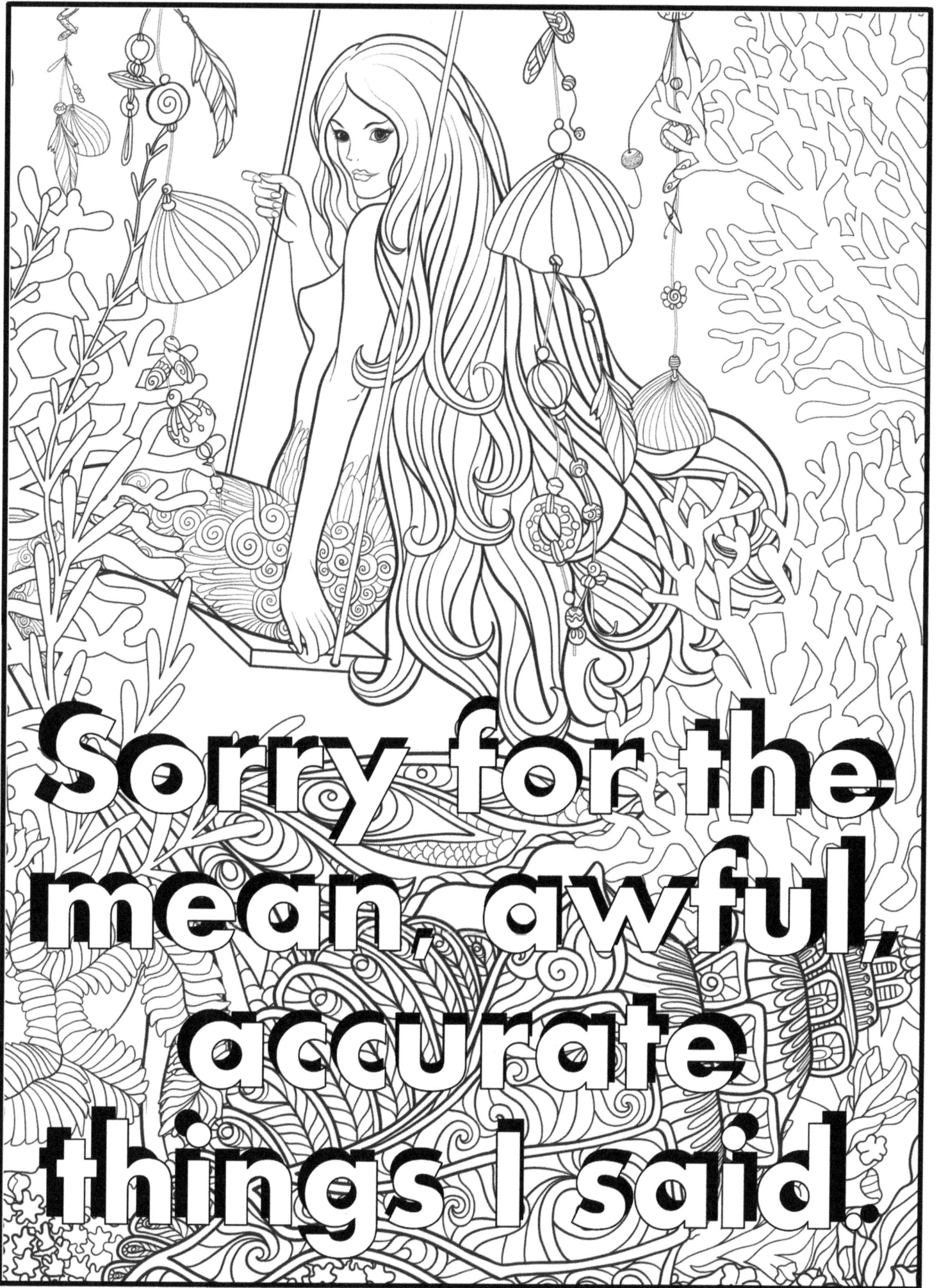

Sorry for the mean, awful, accurate things I said.

if only Closed minds came with Closed mouths

YOU SMELL LIKE DRAMA AND HEADACHE

PLEASE GET AWAY FROM ME

If your phone doesn't ring...

It's me.

WHATEVER

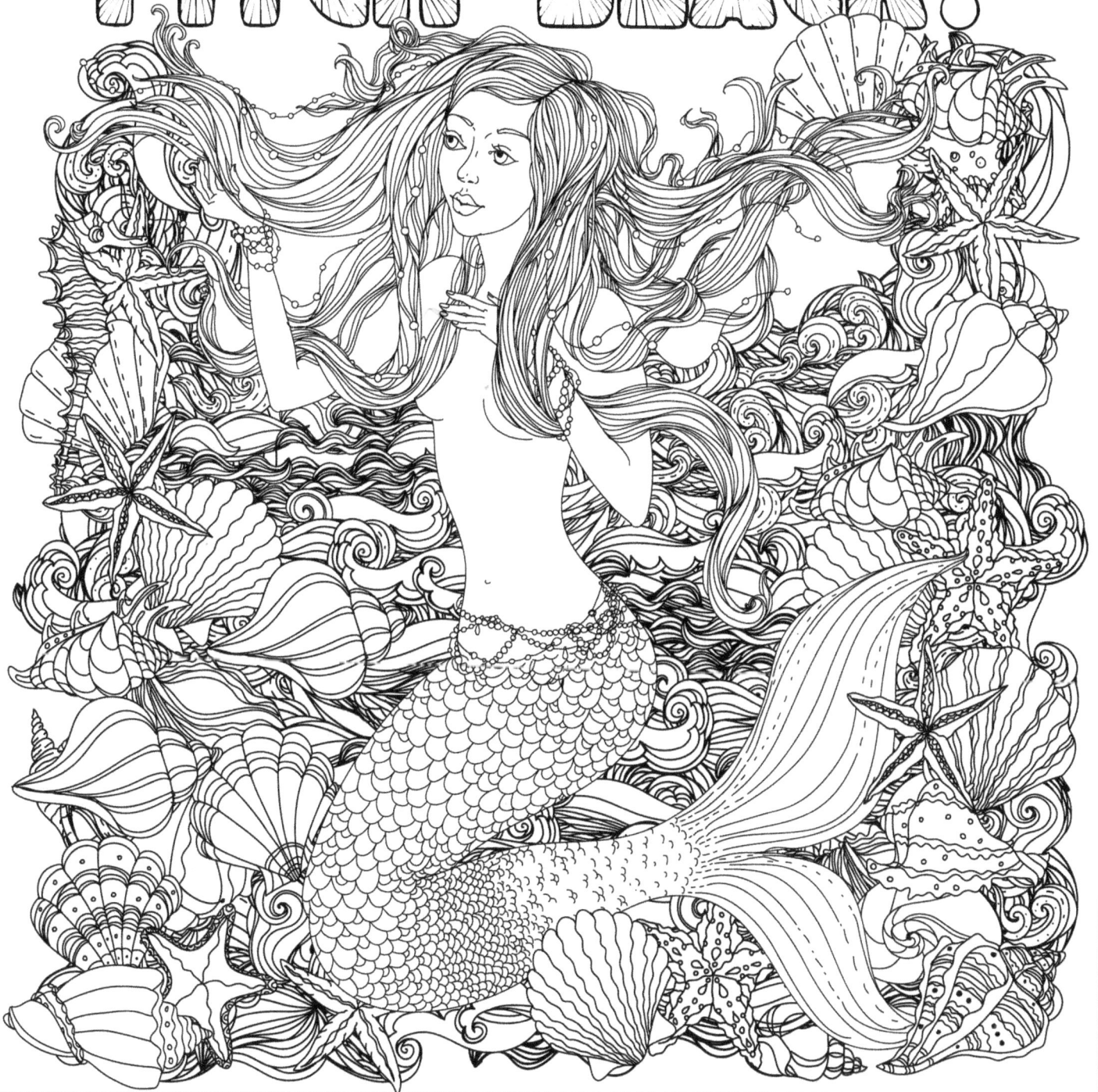

WELL, AREN'T YOU A LITTLE RAY OF PITCH BLACK?

REVENGE IS BENEATH ME.

ACCIDENTS, HOWEVER,

WILL HAPPEN

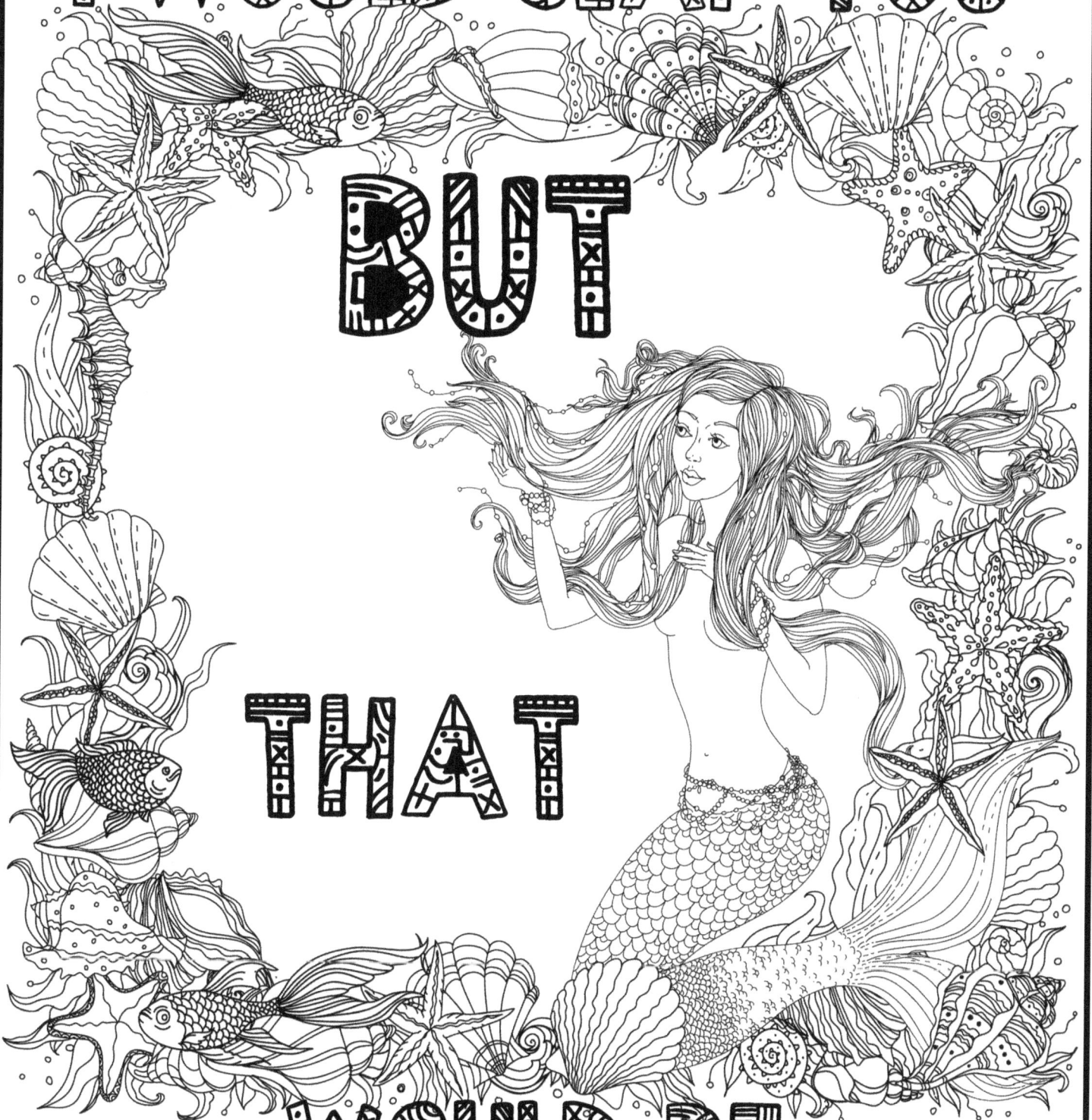

I WOULD SLAP YOU BUT THAT WOULD BE ANIMAL ABUSE

AMAZINGLY ENOUGH,

I DON'T GIVE A SHIT

Someday you'll go far, and I hope you stay there.

YOU ARE OFFENDED BY THE THINGS I SAY?
IMAGINE THE STUFF I HOLD BACK.

SO MUCH TO DO...

SO LITTLE DESIRE TO DO IT

I love the sound you make when you shut up.

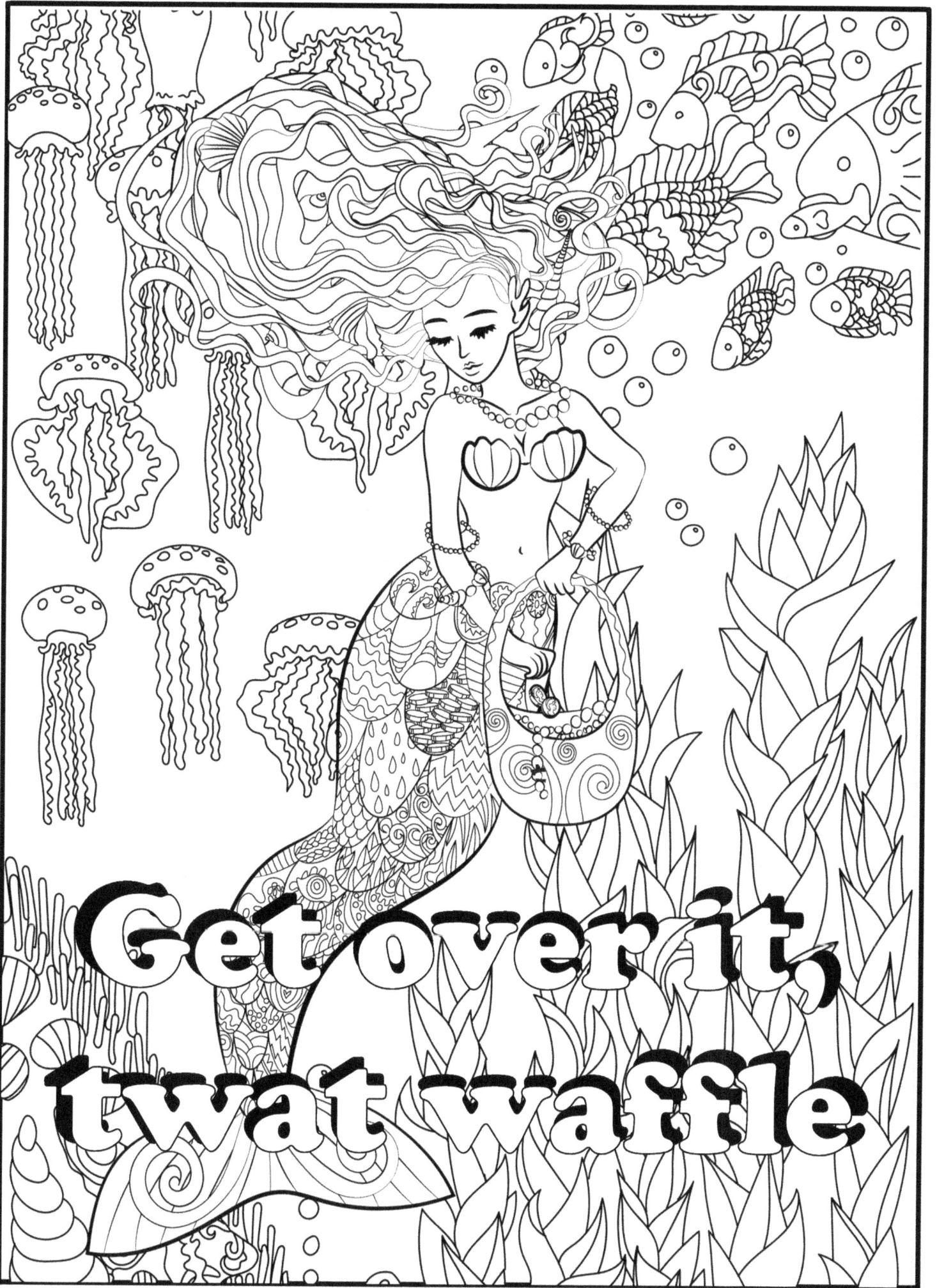

Get over it, twat waffle

NOTHING BRIGHTENS UP A ROOM LIKE YOUR ABSENCE

DON'T MAKE ME
CALL MY FLYING
MONKEYS

Go Fuck Yourself!

BOLLOCKS!

SILENCE IS GOLDEN

DUCT TAPE IS SILVER

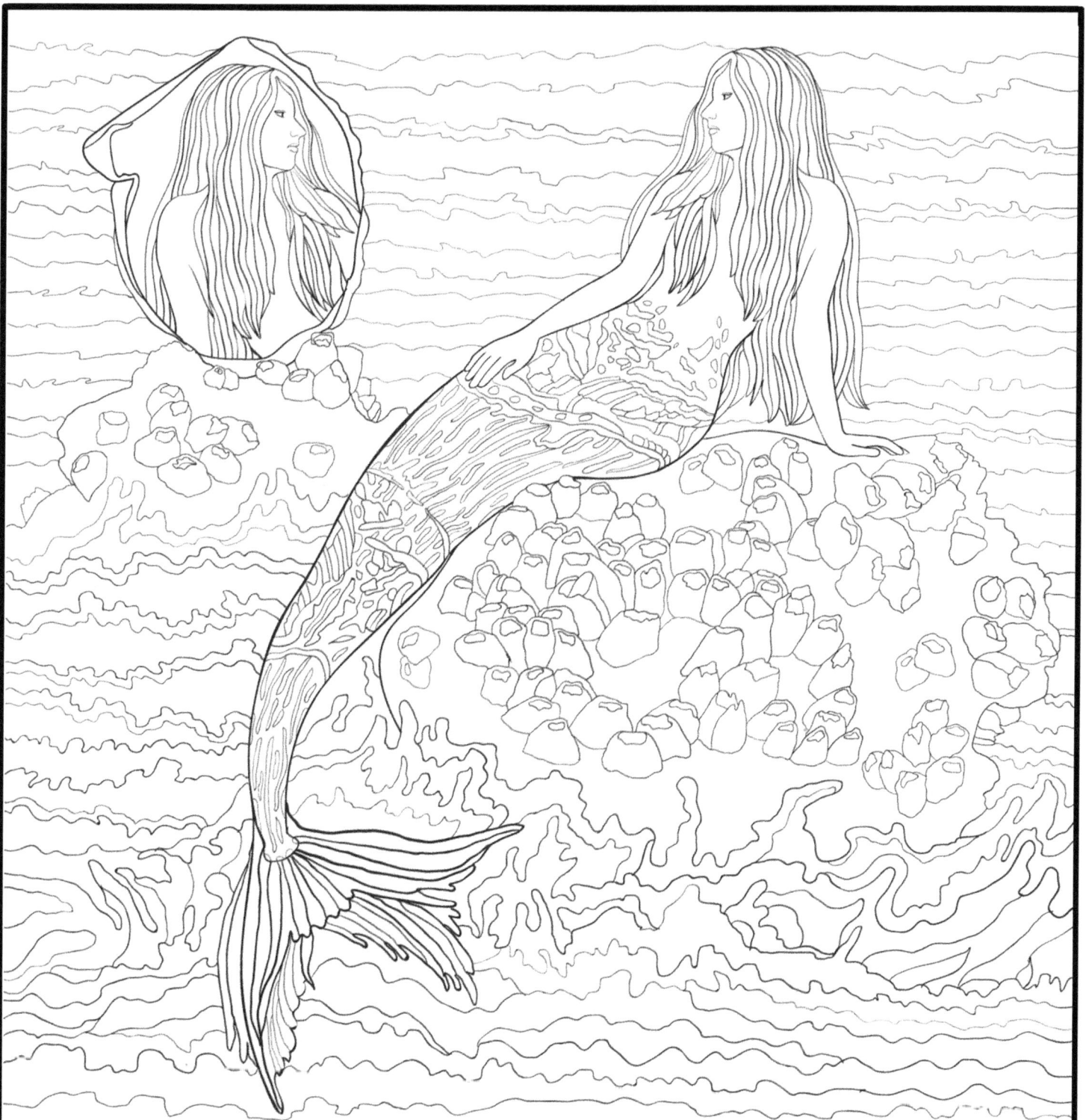

Mirror, mirror, on the fucking rock,
When does the next ocean liner dock?

THIS

is complete
BULLSHIT

ON THIS ROCK DOES DWELL,
THIS USELESS SHELL
FROM HELL.

HOPE YOU
LIKED THIS
BOOK.
KARMA GURU
CREATES
MEANINGFUL
ART FOR YOU.
THANKS FOR
CHOOSING!

www.ingramcontent.com/pod-product-compliance
Lightning Source LLC
Chambersburg PA
CBHW080551030426
42337CB00024B/4839